31 Tips to Healthy Hair

ACHIEVE AND MAINTAIN BEAUTIFUL AND MANAGEABLE HAIR

HAIR CARE SPECIALIST

TISHAWNA D. PRITCHETT

Asia,
You are Beautiful
Blessed & ABLE!

Shawna Pritchett

31 Tips to Healthy Hair: Achieve and Maintain Beautiful and Manageable Hair

Copyright © 2017 Tishawna D. Pritchett

ISBN-13: 978-1976374678

Book cover & Interior Design: TamikaInk.com

Photography by: Connie McGowan, Precise Events & Photography

Acknowledgments

I thank my, Lord and Savior Jesus Christ, for the vision of this book, for using me to share knowledge, for equipping me, and placing amazing people in my life. To my husband, Ron, for the push, your patience and prayers throughout my career and the writing process. You have always encouraged me and never left my side. I love you and appreciate your support. I dedicate this book, my very first book, to you and our daughters, Breona and Ashanti, and granddaughter, Olivia. I am blessed to have the love and support from all of you.

To my mom and dad, Carolyn and Delbert Luster, I love you. To La'Tanyha Boyd thank you for the push. I appreciate the encouragement from you and Tamika Hall throughout this process. To my mentors, educators, clients, family and friends I thank you for every word poured into my life, your support, and your prayers. Lastly, to my pastors, Apostle Michael Hathaway and Prophetess Danielle Hathaway, I love you and thank you for everything that you are to your congregation. Your teachings and prayers lifted me and carried me through to not only finish this book but to start the next one.

TABLE OF CONTENTS

INTRODUCTION

Hair is an extension of your epidermis, the outer layer of your skin and is composed mainly of protein/keratin. The Scalp is layers of skin on the head from which the hair grows. The scalp contains muscles, tissue, sebaceous glands, and the follicles which houses hair strands. To see healthier results with your hair, you should keep your hair and scalp clean, conditioned, and well moisturized. Your ends should be trimmed at least once every eight weeks and regular treatments are necessary as a preventative measure. Most importantly, understanding and actively pursue healthy overall self-care practices is the key to a healthier, better YOU.

There are many misconceptions about what healthy hair actually is. Hair type, texture, color, length, curl pattern, etc. does not determine the health of hair. Healthy hair is hair that has balanced porosity which is the ability to absorb moisture and balanced elasticity the ability to stretch. Healthy hair is also free from split ends, and no breakage.

DON'T PANIC, IT'S NORMAL!

Hair sheds anywhere from 50 to 100 strands daily but can go up to 250 strands daily depending on the stage your hair is in. This is not unusual. This is normal. The process of hair growth is determined by hormones and genetics.

Our hair grows in cycles: Anagen, catagen, and telogen.

- **Anagen** is the active growth stage and is typically determined by genetics but usually lasts anywhere from two to eight years.
- **Catagen** is the transitional stage when Anagen stops before it goes into the resting stage. Catagen typically lasts 2-3 weeks, during which the hair follicle shrinks. (During this time, hair growth is slowing down to prepare for the next stage)
- **Telogen** is the resting stage, which lasts around two to four months. In this stage, the hair is dormant and preparing for a new active growth phase. (This is the stage where hair DOES NOT grow and hair sheds more than the average.)

UNDERSTANDING HAIR LOSS

40% of women experience visible hair loss and most don't notice thinning or the amount that has been lost until 50% is already gone. Some hair loss may be due to an auto immune issue, but most is self-inflicted and can be prevented by better hair care practices. This book will give you 31 tips to help you achieve the hair you desire.

1 Corinthians 6:19-20 (NLT)

Don't you realize that your body is the temple of the Holy Spirit, who lives in you and was given to you by God? You do not belong to yourself, for God bought you with a high price. So you must honor God with your body.

HEALTHY HAIR TIP #1:

GET A PHYSICAL EXAMINATION

Physical Examinations are regular health exams and tests that can help find problems before they start. They also help detect problems early, when your chances for treatment and cure are better. By getting the right health services, screenings, and treatments, you are taking steps that help your chances for living a longer, healthier life.

Understanding your body and what it needs is the beginning of healthy hair. So often as women we see our OB/GYN but many never see a Primary Care Physician for a regular physical. If you haven't gotten yours this year, pick up the phone and schedule a full physical exam today!

Hebrews 10:22

Let us draw near with a sincere heart in full assurance of faith, having our hearts sprinkled clean from an evil conscience and our bodies washed with pure water.

HEALTHY HAIR TIP #2: DETOX

Detox - abstain from or rid the body of toxic or unhealthy substances.

Your hair is an extension of your body. Anything that goes in affects the health of your hair. Think about what you're feeding your mind, body, and spirit.... Is it time to detox, release, and let some things go?

Here are a few quick ways to release toxins from your…

Mind - Try journaling your journey, be better with managing time (get your schedule in order to have a well-balanced life), and/or see a specialist. There is nothing wrong with having a conversation with a therapist, counselor, even your pastor.

Body - Eat cleaner foods, drink plenty of water, and move more. An easy way to identify cleaner foods is looking for dark green leafy vegetables, eat your vegetables as close to a raw state as possible, minimize carbs and sugars, and make your diet colorful. Water and exercise is also essential for a healthy body. Water flushes your system of toxins. See chapter 5 for more about water. Moving more through exercise keeps your heart rate up pumping blood which helps to remove waste.

Our bodies eliminate what it does not need through poop, urine, perspiration and believe it or not, your hair. Everything can be detected through a simple hair strand. This is why court systems are more often using hair for drug testing now more than ever. Your hair tells the truth.

Spirit - Pray, study and meditate on God's word, and fast. Having a prayer partner who is committed to praying and holding you accountable can also be a great benefit.

Stress will happen. How we respond to it is what causes problems.

HEALTHY HAIR TIP #3: STRESS MANAGEMENT

There's good and bad stress that you will encounter in life that can be caused from our thoughts, emotions, schedule, environment and more. This list could go on and on, but here are a few to start:

- Poor time management

- Over worked

- Underpaid

- Preparing for a life change (I.e. wedding, baby, new house, etc.)

- Experiencing a loss (I.e. family, friend, job, etc.)

- Health

- Family dynamics

- Fast-paced lifestyle

- Job

- Ministry

High levels of stress can cause hair to be pushed into a prolonged Telegen (resting) phase. Remember, this is when the follicles are inactive and no growth is present. Control your response to stress by practicing overall self-care for the mind, body, and spirit. Trusting God and having a prayer life has been the greatest stress controller in my life.

HEALTHY HAIR TIP #4: TAKE CARE OF YOUR SCALP

Keep your scalp clean, well moisturized, and free from heavy oils and buildup. It's easier for hair to grow healthy through a clean and healthy scalp. Our scalp produces natural oil on its own. If we follow the regime to keep our scalp moisturized, we would rarely need to add additional oils directly to the scalp.

If adding more oil to the scalp is necessary, please do not use anything based with petroleum. Petroleum is use mainly as a protectant or a blocker. It is not a moisturizer and will clog pores and create a build up around the follicles. If pores are clogged with buildup, it will keep hair from freely flowing. This keeps the hair from having body and bounce. Clogged pores and unhealthy follicles won't allow healthy strands of hair to flow through.

If you want to keep a healthy scalp, remove excessive oils and buildup. In addition, along with massaging the scalp for proper blood flow, manage your diet and water intake are great ways to increase scalp health.

(Protein, Zinc, Iron, Vitamin A, Vitamin B, Vitamin D and others are essentials that promote healthy scalp. The key is knowing when/if there is a deficiency.)

HEALTHY HAIR TIP 5: HYDRATE

Drinking the right amount of water for your body cleanses your organs, flushes away toxins, and adds the right amount of hydration needed for your body type. This allows scalp to be clean and able to produce natural oils so that the scalp is well moisturized and able to grow healthy, shiny, beautiful hair.

There are many suggestions on how to choose the right amount of water for you. You should always consult with your doctor when it comes to health. Until then, just drink water. You can follow the 8x8 rule which is 8, 8oz glasses per day or drinking half of your weight in ounces per day.

HEALTHY HAIR TIP 6: HIRE A PROFESSIONAL HAIRSTYLIST

Knowing how to style at home is great for continuing maintenance, but seeing a professional hairstylist regularly will give you the best results in healthy hair. Assure professionalism so that you are never left in a bind when you really need your hair done, and that stylist doesn't show up or is unprepared to give you what you need.

Wondering what to look for in a stylist? Your stylist should:

- ✓ Has a current license to practice Cosmetology in the state he/she works in.

- ✓ Clean and well groomed.

- ✓ Work space is clean and inviting.

- ✓ Uses barbicide disinfectant for tools.

- ✓ Uses clean towels, capes, tools, etc for each client.

- ✓ Asks questions that will help in choosing the right services for hair health.

- ✓ He/she listens to your concerns and is able to give solid honest feedback.

- ✓ Uses salon exclusive products, not products you can pick up from local beauty supply stores.

- ✓ Is knowledgeable of the products he/she is using.

- ✓ Is honest about service and products being used.

- ✓ Keeps track of appointments using a system. (appointment scheduler or book, not by memory)

- ✓ Acknowledges your presence and makes you feel welcome.

- ✓ You feel comfortable in their space.

- ✓ Understands that your time is just as valuable as theirs.

    - ■ It is very easy to get off track with time in this industry. The smallest thing can cause time to just slip away. If your stylist is negligent with time, then it needs to be brought to their attention that you are not satisfied. Depending on how the stylist replies and/or the future actions, you have a choice to stay or find a new stylist.

HEALTHY HAIR TIP 7: BE HONEST WITH YOUR STYLIST

Build an honest relationship with your professional hairstylist so that he/she can make the best decisions with product choices, styling options, treatment, and advice for at home maintenance. If you are on medication, have been ill, having a medical procedure done, not sleeping well, experiencing a sudden life change, been to another stylist, used chemicals at home, using excessive heat, etc. Your stylist needs to know what's going on with you so that he/she can do what needs to be done and offer suggestions to help and also not use a product or perform a service that may cause a problem. There are some treatments that may cause adverse reactions if used together. Great conversation about life is important to have with your stylist.

HEALTHY HAIR TIP 8: DIET

Take control of your intake to maintain a well-balanced diet to assure you have the nutrients needed for a healthy body. If you are unsure of what you need to add and what you need to decrease, seek professional help.

- See a physician. Go back to tip #1 for help in knowing what you may be deficient in.

- See a nutritionist for assistance with knowing what to eat for your body type. There are many vegetables and fruit options that keep your hair hydrated and well moisturized without having to take the extra vitamins that highly sought after.

- See a Naturopathic specialist for suggestions on what herbs, vitamin and minerals are needed to put in and for suggestions on detoxing for your body.

It all works together for your good!

HEALTHY HAIR TIP 9: IT'S OKAY TO CUT

Have ends trimmed by a professional every eight weeks. If you are getting your ends trimmed on time there should only be a light snipping. Proper maintenance will keep split ends away, allows moisture to be absorbed, and keeps your hair healthy and looking good.

Unless your at home scissors are professional shears sharpened regularly by a professional, you're causing more damage. If you are not getting ends trimmed by a professional or following a suggested maintenance regime, there is a chance that your hair will need a cut and possibly a series of treatments to help with bringing your texture back to normal. Regular trims keep your porosity in balance which helps your hair to maintain its moisture and also keeps the hair looking good with natural body and shine.

HEALTHY HAIR TIP 10: GET TREATMENTS

Hair should be treated regularly as a preventative measure to assure that hair is hydrated properly, and that the PH, elasticity, & porosity are all at a normal level. With this you have healthier, shinier, more manageable beautiful hair. Hair educator, Patrick Bradley explained it best, "You don't take birth control *after* you're pregnant, you take it to *prevent* pregnancy. "

There are many types of treatments for hair and scalp. Depending on your need is what should be given. Your need can be determined but a professional.

HEALTHY HAIR TIP 11: BEWARE OF WOOL

Hair should be treated gently. While your scalp needs the manipulation for blood flow, your hair doesn't like too much activity. The collars on our coats consistently rub around the neckline touching the hair at the nape. Some fabrics, especially wool, is too harsh for our hair and will dry out the hair and eventually hair will snap. Be careful not to have high wool collars. If you do have a high wool collar, consider using silk fashion scarves to block that connection. Wrap the silk scarf around your neck before putting on your coat for that extra protection.

- Fashion tip - Change up the silk/satin scarf periodically to give your winter look some pizzazz!

HEALTHY HAIR TIP 12: ALWAYS SEE A LICENSED COSMETOLOGIST FOR CHEMICALS

To keep hair from being over or under processed, chemicals should be applied by a licensed professional. Cosmetologists are trained and able to determine the correct strength, how long a chemical should stay on, not overlap with previously chemically treated hair, and give you a treatment plan on how to keep your hair healthy.

A licensed professional will evaluate before starting the chemical procedure. A basic pre-chemical evaluation may consist of:

- Porosity check

- Hair density check

- Elasticity check

- Scalp check

- Questions about previous chemical services & lifestyle

I hear comments often that some do their own chemicals at home and there hasn't been a problem. My answer is, not yet. The truth is some may be very knowledgeable and has studied enough to get through their own hair but most have not.

HEALTHY HAIR TIP 13: GET RELAXERS ON TIME

Often times we want to, "stretch out" our relaxers. Doing that without regular maintenance and oversight from a professional stylist may cause problems. Depending on your hair type, you may not be able to wait longer than normal to get a relaxer. See your stylist for professional advice.

If you are getting, "protective styles," in between relaxer services, you may be doing yourself a disservice. Braiding, twisting, and/or constant raveling of your hair strands causes air pockets in the tresses. These pockets cannot absorb moisture as the rest of the hair which cause hair to not look or feel the same texture throughout. Most times when that hair dries, it appears very puffy and dry. This hair is easy to split and thin out. Also, when wearing a straight style, it easily reverts back to natural. This usually causes you to want to add more heat to the hair which will create heat damage resulting in loss of curl pattern or burned hair.

HEALTHY HAIR TIP 14: DON'T BELIEVE EVERYTHING YOU HEAR

Everything that sounds good is not great! Be careful. Companies pay to advertise to those who they believe will buy just because it *sounds* good. They tend to capture us with color, great design, and amazing words we like to hear. Purchasing products or services without research can be a grave mistake. See your stylist for professional advice.

There are many great products on the market. Some are sold in stores as well as the mall or your favorite hair salon. Don't be attracted to scent as much as ingredient. Flip to the next page for some tips on what to look for with ingredients.

●   If you are using a system, stick to the system. The makers of that product has directions listed just for you.

It's easy to choose a product based on smell, texture, popularity, even the design of the container. That normally leads to waste of money, time, and product. I have gathered some information for you to help with choosing what may work for your hair.

* **Essential Oils** - A combined mix of natural oils blended to add moisture and strength for a particular hair texture. Speak with a professional who can help with choosing the right oils (if any needed) and/or other ingredients that your hair may need to treat your hair and scalp for dandruff, dry scalp, itchy scalp, and hair growth.

Here is a list of oils and other ingredients below:

➢ Almond Oil

➢ Argan Oil

➢ Castor Oil

➢ Coconut Oil

➢ Hemp Oil

➢ Jojoba Oil

➢ Olive Oil

➢ Safflower Oil

*Other ingredients

➢ Aloe Vera

➢ BeesWax

➢ Citric Acid

➢ Honey

➢ Pathenol

➢ Peppermint

➢ Rosemary

➢ Shea Butter

The Truth about Allergies

Contact, Environmental, Airborne (Inhaled, and/or Ingested) may play a part in scalp sensitivities which may lead to hairloss.

An allergic reaction can occur when contact is made between an offending allergy and a weakened immune system causing an inflammatory response.

Notes: If you are allergic to tree nuts you may not be able to use products that contains almonds, walnuts, etc. The same goes for peanuts, coconut, oat, castor oil, soy, and other allergy prone ingredients.

TIP 15: PROTECT HAIR FROM THE ENVIRONMENT

The sun, heat, wind, and cold temperatures can dry out hair making it dull and hard to retain moisture. Be sure hair is not just blowing in the wind if so, you're sure to have a tangled, matted mess. Keep hair moisturized and in good condition by covering head with a scarf or hat when going outside in the weather. As always, it's best to use a satin or silk material for hair coverings. See tip #16 for suggestions on how to choose the best hat.

HEALTHY HAIR TIP 16: CHECK THE LINING

INSIDE YOUR HAT

When it's COLD, you WILL need a hat. Brrrr... If your hat is not lined with satin, silk, or a smooth material that will allow your hair to slide and not snag, use a wig cap or a satin bonnet under your hat. Make sure that the bonnet is a clean one. NOT the one you had on last night. The bonnet MUST be removed immediately when you get to your destination. Contrary to popular belief, bonnets are not a fashion piece and were never created for such, LOL. They can be an easy grab and go, but it is not a great fashion statement, and is not the best sanitary option.

HEALTHY HAIR TIP 17: CORRECT COMB CHOICE

A wide tooth comb can be used to detangle and style hair. Using small combs at home should only be used for parting or smoothing areas while styling if necessary. If you must shampoo at home, there are combs and brushes made especially for wet hair. Be sure to invest in them. Always see your stylist for professional advice.

HEALTHY HAIR TIP 18: MASSAGE SCALP

Regular scalp massage is necessary to enhance blood circulation and scalp pliability. Without the circulation of blood in the scalp, it's impossible to keep healthy follicles. Without scalp pliability, there's no way for moisture to be retained. This all causes dryness and hair loss. Massage daily using the balls of your fingertips, going in light and soft circular motions throughout your head including neck, behind ears, and temples. This has been known to knock out a headache as well. Try it!

HEALTHY HAIR TIP 19: TAKE A BREAK FROM WEAVE

We are not our hair... Wearing a weave is never a requirement, it's a choice and not a necessity. However, some drastic issues with health and hair does causes some to turn to weave or wigs. There are also those who enjoy giving their hair a break and wearing a weave for a period of time or wearing one for a special occasion. These are okay, but there are precautions to take when choosing weaves or a wig.

Get a consultation from your stylist to assure that you are making the best decision. Your consultation should include what's being done, how it's being done, how long it will stay in, what type of hair that will be used, and what will regular maintenance consist of. Too tight, too heavy, technique, not caring for your own hair while wearing a weave and keeping your weave in too long, are major causes of hair breakage due to wearing a one.

HEALTHY HAIR TIP 20: HAVE A CONVERSATION WITH YOUR BRAIDER

If it hurts, it may be causing a problem. Braids that are too tight and too heavy will cause scalp irritation and damage follicles. Also, make sure you are not allergic to the hair that is being used and its not an irritant to your skin and scalp. Technique also plays a major role in hair breakage due to getting hair braided. Depending on your hair type, texture, and condition your braider should be able to determine the best style or technique of braids to keep your hair in good condition and your edges in tact. Have that sometime uncomfortable but courageous conversation with the person who is braiding your hair. Ultimately, the effects affects you!

Psalm 139:14New King James Version (NKJV)

14 I will praise You, for I am
fearfully and wonderfully made;[a]
Marvelous are Your works,
And that my soul knows very well.

HEALTHY HAIR TIP 21: STOP COMPARING

Your physical make up, what's on your mind, and how you're feeling won't ever be the same as the next person which means your hair won't ever do what the next person's hair does. It is easy to say what your family member or friend can do with their hair and wonder why you can't. Just remember, although with family we may be genetically connected, we are not the same. We are all uniquely created in God's image. HE knows the very hairs on our heads but HE never said they will all be the same.

Embrace your uniqueness and your own beauty. Be confident in yourself and the God you serve.

Genesis 1:27King James Version (KJV)

27 So God created man in his own image, in the image of God created he him; male and female created he them.

HEALTHY HAIR TIP 22: CARE ABOUT YOUR EDGES

The hair around your edges is the most fragile hair on your head and should be handled more gently than any other hair. The material on your head ties and hats, wearing braids, weaves, ponytails, some updos, not properly relaxing hair, using rubber bands and hair ties pulled too tightly, consistently wearing headbands, even bonnets and wig caps are just a few ways that hairloss can happen around your edges. Also, know that some medications, stress, and health concerns will cause hairloss. Drastic and sudden weight loss and weight gain in most cases causes hair loss and typically is seen around the hairline and crown area of the head before anywhere else. The stress from the sudden weight loss or gain can send the follicles into the resting phase causing extreme shedding. This can also happen with medical conditions such as high fevers and childbirth.

Seek advice from a professional, always.

HEALTHY HAIR TIP 23: CHECK YOUR COMBS

Did you know that you can split and/or break your hair by using old combs? If a comb has a broken tooth, is bent up, has a split or scratched it should be thrown away. That damaged tool can cause damage to the hair. Choose quality tools when purchasing items for your hair. Anytime you use heat, be sure to use tools that can withstand it. Always keep them clean and in good condition. When visiting a salon or having someone else do your hair it's okay to check their combs to assure they are clean and in good condition. If there is a problem with being asked to look then that's a sign that you shouldn't be there. A professional is confident enough in what they are doing to not be intimidated when you ask.

HEALTHY HAIR TIP 24: FALL IN LOVE WITH

SATIN AND SILK

Hair will slide against real satin and silk and not snag hair unlike many other materials like wool, some cotton, polyester, etc. that may dry out and eventually break hair. Silk feels good against the skin and works wonders on the hair. There are cheaper versions in some stores. Please do not be fooled. Wash it one time and it's no good. Remember, you get what you pay for.

Save time and money by purchasing quality wraps, bonnets, scarfs, and hats for your hair.

HEALTHY HAIR TIP 25: WASH YOUR HEAD WRAPS

The same day you shampoo your hair, you should wash your head wraps, combs, brushes, etc. before using them on your clean hair. Don't make the mistake of wrapping a perfectly good style, at night then waking the next morning to find your hair being greasy and smelly because you didn't change your scarf and/or pillow case.

Using the correct head wraps is just as important. Remember, satin and silk are friends to your hair!

HEALTHY HAIR TIP 26: REMOVE WEAVE WISELY

The professional who installs your weave should be the same one to remove it. There are many techniques to installing a weave and the best removal technique should be followed by the directions of how it was installed.

Have a conversation with your professional prior to having the install done to assure the removal process is understood.

Incorrect removal may cause, thinning hair, hair breakage, split ends, scalp irritation, and follicle damage.

<u>HEALTHY HAIR TIP 27: BEWARE OF HEAT</u>

Using too much heat on your hair can cause damage. Excessive heat can cause hair to be burned, scorched, dried out, split, and lifeless. When heat exceeds 400 degrees on the healthiest head of hair, there's a chance of this damage happening as well. There are tools that can be used to help in keeping hair from being exposed to too much direct heat such as the plates on your flat iron, temperature setting, types of blow dryer used, using the correct brush and a heat protectant. Do not curl or flat iron dirty hair or hair that is weak and shows sign of damage. As always, seek the advice from your professional Cosmetologist for help in choosing the right tool and style for you.

HEALTHY HAIR TIP 28: TALK ABOUT IT

Once again, stress can cause great damage to your hair. If you find yourself at wits end, seek counseling from someone other than your regular circle. Talk to a professional counselor, therapist, pastor, and/or mentor. Everyone needs to discuss life and issues to be able release (sometimes forgive) and move on with joy.

The ability to converse with others is more important than most people believe. Truth is, effective communication is the most important of all life skills.

HEALTHY HAIR TIP 29: HAVE FUN!

The Bible tells us that laughter is good for the soul. It's also good for the hair! We are in total control of our mood. Let's laugh, engage in great conversation, and enjoy life. How we deal with our emotional health is very important to our physical health which all shows in our hair health.

HEALTHY HAIR TIP 30: FOLLOW A HAIR MAINTENANCE SCHEDULE.

Ask your stylist to help you write out your own regimen to follow for your hair care. This will include how often you shampoo, when to get treatments, trim ends, what products to use and how often, water intake, when and how to massage the scalp, changing up your style, and more.

HEALTHY HAIR TIP 31: TAKE CARE OF YOU

Our hair is typically a reflection of how we care for ourselves. If you do too much of anything, it reflects in your hair. If you don't do enough of anything, it reflects in your hair. So often, we are caring for everyone else and forget about ourselves, then we look in the mirror and become sad, disappointed, and sometimes angry.

➢ Let's take time for ourselves.

➢ Let's choose to be a priority in our own lives.

➢ Let's write out our goals.

➢ Let's pursue our passion.

➢ Let's learn to say NO sometimes.

➢ Let's go after the things that our heart desires.

➢ Let's love the person God created us to be.

➢ Let's trust God more.

A QUICK GUIDE TO AVOIDING HAIRLOSS

Stress & Poor Hair Care Regimen

Your reaction to good and/or bad stress can cause hair loss. Too much of anything can cause problems.

Diet

Maintain a well-balanced diet. Dull, lifeless hair is often a sign of poor diet. Avoid fad diets and learn to eat to live. Vitamins, minerals, and herbs may be needed as an added benefit. See a physician or nutritionist for guidance.

Health/Hormonal Imbalance

Your hormones can stimulate hair growth and hair loss. Poor vitamin assimilation, Pregnancy, Menopause, over/underactive thyroid, etc are all health concerns that may cause hair loss.

Medication/Illness

Most mood stabilizers and antidepressants can cause hair loss. Seek advice from a medical professional.

Androgenetic Alopecia

Also known as Hereditary or female/male pattern hair loss. There are many types of Alopecia. You may seek advice from a professional who studies hair and scalp and understands the growth cycle.

See Your Stylist Regularly

Find a professional stylist who is knowledgeable about hair care. Be open and honest with them and give them an opportunity to get to know you and your hair.

Exercise

Exercise increases the blood circulation in the body which will result in nourishment of the hair follicles, resulting in healthier hair

Stress Management

Taking charge of you! Your thoughts, emotions, schedule, environment, and the way you deal with your problems.

Seek professional help if needed:

Cosmetologist - a licensed expert in the care of hair, skin, and makeup.

Dermatologist - a medical expert who treats diseases and cosmetic problems of the skin and scalp.

Trichologist - one who studies and practices the science of hair and scalp.

Physician - medical expert who is able to diagnosis and treat injuries and illnesses.

Therapist - a human services expert in the area of council to eliminate and/or minimize stress.

Pastor - the spiritual leader over a group of people furthering the work of the church while leading others into a growing relationship with Christ.

BONUS: SHAWN'S 10 STEP MORNING SELF-CARE REGIMEN.

This is a great start to making my day amazing. You're welcome to try it!

1. Start your morning with prayer. Let the first conversation of your day be with God.

2. Read your morning devotional and write in your journal.

3. Allow time to study, meditate, and pray on the scripture in the message of your morning.

4. Take time for praise and thanksgiving.

5. Drink at least 8 ounces of water in the morning before food or coffee. (Warm lemon water preferred)

6. Do a full body stretch and walk (and/or workout). Follow the directions of a professional who can help with your needs.

7. Eat breakfast. Whether it is a full breakfast or just fruit and toast, eat breakfast.

8. Write out your top 3 goals for the day.

9. Look in the mirror and tell yourself that you are Beautiful, Blessed, and ABLE!

10. Go make the best of the day and remember it is already blessed. It's up to you to make it amazing!

ABOUT THE AUTHOR

A mother, daughter, sister, wife, neighbor, and friend...Tishawna is a Licensed Professional Hair Care Specialist and Board Certified Cosmetology Instructor, specializing in preventative care and hair restoration for women.

She is the owner of Shawn's Hair N More, Hair Restoration Studio and Styling Salon in Henrico, VA. To name a few, her work can be seen in Essence Magazine Hot Hair Edition, Black Beauty Hairstyling Magazine, Extreme Hairstyle Magazine, Jet, and Sophisticate's Black Hair Magazine where she is a featured stylist giving expert advice for their annual Trend Report. Tishawna has been featured on Channel 8 news as an expert on haircare. She has trained with the best in the industry traveling across the US to get the best of the best including advance technical training and Trichology, the science of hair and scalp. At Shawn's Hair N More, she provides quality hair & scalp services that restore and maintain the natural health, beauty, and shine that the client's hair deserves. Tishawna has worked as a technical educator with Ashtae Products and Black Beauty Expo, she attended Innovations Today School of Trichology with Rodney Barnett, advanced studies at Beauty SuperStars with Miki Wright, and has served as educator with Beauty Expo, Empire Beauty, as well as contracted trainer at local schools, salons, and summer camps. She has been a member of Black Beauty Association, National Cosmetology Association, training with Michael Cole's Summit Salon Business, a graduate of Kingdom Entreprenuer University with Tiphani Montgomery and founder of ABLE Conversations - Stylist Edition. Tishawna frequently attends classes, workshops, expos, private trainings, and beauty summits to stay connected and advanced as a business and beauty professional.

Working with women daily helped Tishawna to find her true purpose. Seeing the joys & laughter, the tears & pain, also her own life's experiences pushed her closer to accept the call to do something. Tishawna founded A Beautiful Lady Exploration Center better known as The ABLE Center, a non-profit organization that serves as an advocate for the Everyday Working Woman, providing resources and services that motivate, empower, and equip everyday working women to become better mothers, daughters, sisters, wives, neighbors, and friends. Through their solutions focused workshops, events, and reliable resources, they are committed to being and helping those who desire to be "A Better Me" physically, mentally, emotionally, spiritually, and socially for overall self-care.

Tishawna has overcome many obstacles to include low self-esteem, social anxiety, and emotional exhaustion. She gives all thanks, honor, and glory to God for delivering her and equipping her to be able to help others to believe in themselves and walk boldly and unapologetically in their divine purpose. Tishawna believes that women deserve another chance and she believes even more that love never fails. A common quote from her is, "It's time to help women to be better so that our families can be better, which will result in our communities being better, making this world a better place."

For more with Tishawna (speaking engagements, workshops, training) visit her website at:
www.TishawnaPritchett.com